Remotely operated shutoff valves (ROSOVs

for emergency isolation of hazardous substances

Guidance on good practice

HSE BOOKS

Contents

Introduction 1
What is a remotely operated shutoff valve? 1
Who is this guidance for? 1
Why is there a need for guidance? 1
Lessons from the Associated Octel fire 1
HSE response 2
How HSE uses good practice in assessing compliance 2
How to use this guidance 3
Meeting the standard 4
ALARP demonstration 4

Scope of the guidance 5
Hazardous substances included 5
Activities included 5
Topics excluded 6

Assessing your site 7
Hierarchy of measures 7
New installations 7
Existing installations 7
Reasonable practicability 7
Precautionary approach 8
When to consider fitting a ROSOV 8
Benefits of ROSOVs 8
Personal protective equipment 8
Bunding 9
Dual hazard substances and mixtures 9

The selection criteria 10
How do the selection criteria work? 10
The primary selection criteria 10
The secondary selection criteria 11

Selection and operation of ROSOVs 12
Activation 12
Types of valves 12
Actuators 12
Failure mode 12
External hazards 13
Consequential hazards 13
Dual function valves 13
Excess flow valves 13
Reliability and integrity 14

Appendix 1 A case-specific assessment of the reasonable practicability of a ROSOV 15

Appendix 2 Summary of relevant legal requirements 29

References and useful addresses 30

Introduction

What is a remotely operated shutoff valve?

1. In this guidance a remotely operated shutoff valve (ROSOV) is defined as:

   - A valve designed, installed and maintained for the primary purpose of achieving rapid isolation of plant items containing hazardous substances in the event of a failure of the primary containment system (including, but not limited to, leaks from pipework, flanges, and pump seals). Closure of the valve can be initiated from a point remote from the valve itself. The valve should be capable of closing and maintaining tight shutoff under foreseeable conditions following such a failure (which may include fire).

2. Valves performing the same or similar function may also be referred to as: emergency isolation valves (EIVs); remotely-operated block valves (RBVs); or emergency shutdown valves (ESDVs).

3. This guidance will help you identify the need for remote isolation of hazardous substances using ROSOVs, as part of your emergency arrangements for the safe and controlled shutdown of plant and equipment.

Who is this guidance for?

4. This guidance is issued by the Health and Safety Executive (HSE) to assist duty holders in complying with relevant health and safety law. Following the guidance is not compulsory and you are free to take other **equally effective action**.

5. The guidance is for operators and managers of hazardous installations handling, storing or processing the hazardous substances detailed in the scope. It will also be of interest to plant supervisors, design, process, and maintenance engineers and safety professionals.

6. Throughout this guidance references to the implementation of a ROSOV should be taken to mean a ROSOV or other equally effective measures that will achieve an equivalent degree of risk reduction. All published material is listed in the References and useful addresses section and titles appear in *italics*.

Why is there a need for guidance?

7. In an emergency, rapid isolation of vessels or process plant is one of the most effective means of preventing loss of containment, or limiting its size.

8. This guide gives you simplified criteria for deciding when you need to provide a facility for remote isolation.

9. The appendices include guidance on how to make a case-specific assessment of the reasonable practicability of retrofitting a ROSOV to an existing installation.

10. The provision of ROSOVs was highlighted by the HSE investigation into an incident at the Associated Octel Company Limited at Ellesmere Port in February 1994. The findings of the investigation into this incident were published by HSE in 1996: *The chemical release and fire at the Associated Octel Company Limited*.[1]

11. Another incident that has contributed to the drive for guidance on ROSOVs was the fire on the fluidised bed catalytic cracking unit at the BP Grangemouth Refinery in June 2000. A report on the incident is available on the HSE website on www.hse.gov.uk/comah/bpgrange/contents.htm

Lessons from the Associated Octel fire

12. One of the conclusions of the Associated Octel report was that the incident escalated rapidly because it was not possible to stop the initial release. This problem could have been avoided if ROSOVs had been installed (as they were elsewhere on the site). The report described a number of lessons to be learned from the incident including the following, which relate directly to the provision of ROSOVs:

   '**Lesson 5**: As part of their comprehensive risk assessments, companies in control of chemical process plant at major hazards sites should critically review the provision of ROSOVs at both storage and process vessels in which significant inventories of dangerous substances are held.

1

Lesson 6: HSE, in conjunction with other interested parties, should develop and publish additional guidance on the provision of ROSOVs and other methods of mitigating risks on process plant.'

HSE response

13. In response to Lesson 6, interim guidance on the general principles of isolation of hazardous substances was published by HSE: Chemicals Information Sheet No 2 *Emergency isolation of process plant in the chemical industry*.[2]

How HSE uses good practice in assessing compliance

14. The law requires that you undertake a suitable and sufficient risk assessment to determine the measures necessary to ensure that risks to health and safety are adequately controlled.

15. HSE expects suitable controls to be in place to address every significant hazard and that as a **minimum** those controls must achieve the standard of recognised good practice precautions for your industry.

16. HSE inspectors seek to secure compliance with the law and may refer to relevant codes, standards and guidance as illustrating good practice.

17. HSE's publication *Reducing risks, protecting people* (R2P2)[3] and the supporting document *Assessing compliance with the law in individual cases and the use of good practice*[4] discuss HSE's policy on the role of good practice. The latter includes a definition of good practice in this context. Both are available on the HSE website at www.hse.gov.uk

18. Adopting relevant good practice precautions for your industry is a straightforward way to demonstrate that you are controlling risks effectively. It frees you from the need to take explicit account of the costs and benefits of each individual risk control measure (system of work, item of hardware etc). These will have been considered when the good practice was established. However, this does not mean that you will never need to do any more to satisfy the law. You still have a duty to consider if there is anything about your circumstances that means further action is necessary.

19. HSE considers that this guidance represents good practice for emergency isolation within the limitations of the scope. However, the guidance is under continuous review and advances in technology or new knowledge of hazards may lead HSE inspectors to seek a higher standard in some cases – the standard set here should, therefore, be regarded as the minimum.

How to use this guidance

20. The flowchart in Figure 1 summarises how to apply this guidance to identify where ROSOVs should be provided.

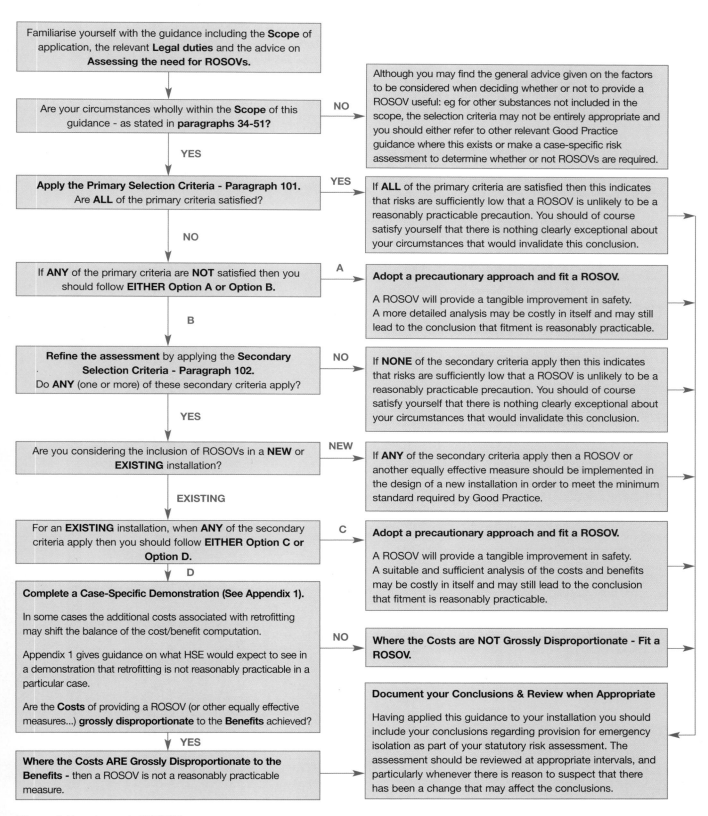

Figure 1 *How to apply ROSOVs*

Meeting the standard

21. You should compare the provision for emergency isolation on your site against the selection criteria and identify any areas where the precautions in place do not meet the standard described in this guidance.

22. Unless the selection criteria indicate otherwise, ROSOVs should be incorporated into the design of a new installation.

23. In the case of an existing installation ROSOVs should be provided unless you can demonstrate that retrofitting is not 'reasonably practicable' in the circumstances (see Appendix 1).

24. A phased, prioritised programme of upgrading may be appropriate. If necessary you can discuss with the HSE proposed work arising from your assessments. Where you consider that you have identified alternative but equally (or more) effective means to control the risk you should document these conclusions as part of the record of your statutory risk assessment.

25. This risk assessment needs to be kept under review. Changes in understanding of the risk, or reductions in the costs of implementing the measure, may shift the balance of the cost/benefit equation.

26. Following this good practice guidance does not mean you will need **additional** documented demonstrations of safety. If you use other equally effective measures instead of a ROSOV, there is no need to perform a separate assessment. Your demonstration that the measures actually in place make risks as low as reasonably practicable (ALARP) is all that is needed.

27. If you cannot demonstrate that you have other equally effective measures on site and you do not have a ROSOV where one is indicated by this guidance then you should be able to show that fitting a ROSOV is not reasonably practicable.

28. Appendix 1 of this guidance gives additional advice on demonstrating reasonable practicability. Appendix 2 summarises some of the relevant legal requirements relating to the recording of risk assessment findings in general and the more detailed requirements imposed on some duty holders under the *Control of Major Accident Hazards Regulations 1999* (COMAH).[5]

29. If a detailed risk assessment shows that upgrading is not reasonably practicable then the basis for this conclusion should be documented as part of your assessment record.

ALARP demonstration

30. This guidance is limited to a consideration of a single risk reduction measure – the provision for emergency isolation. This may be only one of a number of measures necessary to make the risk from a particular hazard ALARP.

31. Where it can be shown that conformance with good practice results in risks being reduced to the 'broadly acceptable' level (see *R2P2*)[3] then this will normally be accepted as demonstrating compliance with the law.

32. Where the residual risk remains higher, in the 'ALARP region' (*R2P2*)[3] then you should continue to seek further reasonably practicable risk reduction measures and, where applicable, to include these as part of your ALARP demonstration.

33. Good practice that covers all the risks from your work activity may not be available, so if you are required to make an explicit ALARP demonstration, a more rigorous analysis may be needed to demonstrate that all measures necessary have been implemented.

Scope of the guidance

Hazardous substances included

34. This guidance is limited to operations involving the storage, transfer, or processing of substances that are:

   - classified under the *Chemicals (Hazard Information and Packaging for Supply) Regulations 2002* (CHIP)[6] as flammable, highly flammable, extremely flammable, toxic or very toxic; and
   - liquids or gases under the conditions of storage and/or processing.

35. The general advice on what you should consider when deciding whether or not to provide a ROSOV may also be useful in the context of other hazardous substances. However, these other substances were not considered in setting the decision criteria and so the specific result might not be appropriate in every case.

36. When deciding if you need to provide ROSOVs for substances not included in the scope of this guidance, you should either:

   - refer to other good practice guidance written for that substance or category of substances; or
   - undertake your own case-specific risk assessment.

37. Appendix 1 is a useful guide for making a case-specific risk assessment. However, you will need to consider explicitly the hazardous properties (physical, chemical and toxicological) of the substances you use if the risk assessment is to be suitable and sufficient.

38. Some higher flashpoint substances not classified under CHIP as flammable are stored or processed at temperatures above their flashpoint, or under elevated pressures. These may be capable of forming a flammable atmosphere following loss of containment. This guidance will also be useful in deciding whether or not to provide for remote isolation of substances in this category where more specific guidance does not currently exist.

39. Some substances will not be included in the current CHIP *Approved supply list*,[7] which lists dangerous chemicals along with their EC-agreed classifications. This may include intermediates that are not 'supplied' and, therefore, would not be subject to CHIP. To apply this guidance you will need to self-classify the substance according to the method described in the CHIP *Approved classification and labelling guide*[6] as if it were intended for supply.

40. Some substances may have dual classification. For substances with both flammable and toxic properties each hazard should be assessed separately. If different standards are indicated then the higher standard should be adopted.

41. This guidance may lead you to conclude that a ROSOV is not a reasonably practicable measure for the control of risks to health and safety. However, the Environment Agency (EA) or the Scottish Environment Protection Agency (SEPA) may still require you to provide for remote isolation of dangerous substances to protect the environment. For details of how to contact the EA and SEPA see References and useful addresses section.

Activities included

Onshore installations

42. This guidance is applicable at onshore installations including chemical manufacturing sites, petrochemical facilities and sites engaged in the storage and distribution (excluding long distance pipelines) of hazardous substances.

43. The guidance may be applied at all onshore facilities where storage, transfer or processing of the specified categories of substances takes place, irrespective of whether the site is subject to the requirements of COMAH.

Petroleum dispensing

44. Petroleum retail is subject to a licensing regime and is outside of the scope of this guidance. The provision of technical measures including means of safe isolation in an emergency is covered by specific guidance and, where appropriate, by licence conditions.

45. However, this guidance is applicable where the non-retail dispensing of fuel into vehicles takes place, eg during vehicle manufacture.

Offshore installations and transmission pipelines (on or offshore)

46. This guidance was produced specifically for use by the onshore sector. Offshore installations, and pipelines covered by the *Pipelines Safety Regulations 1996*,[8] are subject to specific legislation that includes explicit requirements for remote operation of plant, including emergency shutdown valves. For example, the *Offshore Installations (Prevention of Fire and Explosion, and Emergency Response) Regulations 1995* (regulation 12)[9] and the *Pipelines Safety Regulations 1996* (regulation 19).[8]

Topics excluded

47. This guidance does not give detailed advice on measures for process control or pressure relief arrangements (including reactor depressurisation and the 'dumping' or 'quenching' of runaway reactions) and the following issues are excluded.

Specification of valves

48. Advice on suitability of valves to perform a particular duty, including appropriate materials of construction, should be sought from your supplier or manufacturer.

Maintenance

49. It is frequently necessary to isolate plant containing hazardous substances to allow for maintenance. The requirements for safe isolation for these purposes are not covered here. Advice on this topic may be found in HSE's *The safe isolation of plant and equipment*.[10]

Detection systems

50. This guidance does not consider in any detail the detection systems that are a necessary component of a system for automatic activation of ROSOVs (automatic shutoff valves, ASOVs).

Control of exothermic reactions

51. There is a role for remotely operated valves in the control and emergency shutdown of exothermic reactions to avoid runaway. The use of ROSOVs for these purposes is outside of the scope of this guidance, but advice can be found in the HSE publication *Designing and operating safe chemical reaction processes*.[11]

Assessing your site

Hierarchy of measures

52. You should be able to demonstrate that you have considered a hierarchy of measures:

    - Inherently safer options (such as substitution of a hazardous substance by a less hazardous one, reducing the quantity of the substance stored or processed etc).
    - Options for prevention and control of loss of containment (such as preventive maintenance, inspection, testing etc).
    - Mitigation measures (such as ROSOVs and bunding).

53. For existing installations, options for inherently safer processes will be more limited. You should still give priority to measures that prevent or limit loss of the hazardous substance from the primary containment over mitigation measures such as secondary containment.

54. The guidance applies to both new and existing installations.

New installations

55. The design of a new installation should fully conform to the good practice set out in this guidance.

Existing installations

56. For existing installations where the current provision does not meet the standard set out in this guidance, you should upgrade the installation so far as is reasonably practicable. Take your current situation as the starting point, when you assess the risk to be reduced, for comparison with the cost of achieving that reduction. You may take account of any measures that are already in place when establishing the present level of risk (without a ROSOV). However, the measures must be effective against the same containment failures, for example:

    - where items of plant are bunded there may be long runs of interconnecting pipework outside the bund;
    - a ROSOV close to the plant item will provide protection wherever a pipework failure occurs but bunding will only mitigate releases that occur within the bunded area.

57. It is recognised that there may be additional costs associated with retrofitting measures to existing installations and that it is appropriate to consider these extra costs when reaching a decision on reasonable practicability. In *R2P2*[3] Appendix 3 includes a discussion of the relevant cost and benefits to be considered.

58. Some of the additional costs associated with retrofitting, such as downtime and loss of production, can be minimised by co-ordinating the retrofitting with planned maintenance, refurbishment or upgrading of the installation.

Reasonable practicability

59. HSE considers that duties to ensure health and safety so far as is reasonably practicable (SFAIRP) and duties to reduce risks as low as is reasonably practicable (ALARP) are equivalent. Each calls for the same set of tests to be applied.

60. The requirement under COMAH to take 'all measures necessary' to prevent major accidents and limit their consequences is interpreted as meaning that the risks from major accident hazards should be reduced to ALARP.

61. In some circumstances the risks from a particular hazardous activity may be so high as to be unacceptable for all practical purposes, whatever the associated level of benefits. Conversely, when the level of risk is inherently very low or has been made very low by the application of suitable controls, then for most practical purposes the risk can be regarded as insignificant. HSE would not normally seek further risk reduction measures, as the resource required would be disproportionate to the risk. However, where further reasonably practicable risk reduction measures can be identified then the law requires that these be implemented.

62. Between these two extremes, a given level of risk from a hazardous activity may be judged **tolerable** for the benefits that the activity brings, provided that the risk is made ALARP.

63. Where the risks are **tolerable, if ALARP** you should compare:

    - the benefits arising from the reduction in risk achieved by particular measures; and
    - the cost in time, money or trouble of implementing those measures.

64. Only where there is a 'gross disproportion' between the two, ie the risk reduction being insignificant in relation to the cost, can the measures be ruled out as **not** reasonably practicable.

65. Further discussion of the tolerability of risk and the principle of ALARP can be found in the HSE publication *R2P2*.[3]

Precautionary approach

66. When making decisions regarding the provision of risk reduction measures it is HSE policy to adopt more cautious estimates:

   - whenever there is good reason to believe that serious harm might occur, even if the likelihood is remote; or
   - when uncertainty regarding either the consequences or the likelihood undermines confidence in the conclusions of the risk assessment.

   (Serious harm is defined as death or serious personal injury, especially when multiple casualties result from a single event.)

When to consider fitting a ROSOV

67. You should assess the need to fit a ROSOV wherever there is the potential for a major accident as a result of loss of containment of a hazardous substance, the consequences of which could be significantly reduced by rapid isolation.

68. Manual valves should **never** be used in situations where the employee effecting the isolation would be placed in danger. This is a major consideration in deciding when to use ROSOVs. Manual valve isolation may be acceptable in some cases where rapid isolation is not required to prevent a major accident. However, manual valves are often fitted mainly for maintenance work and are unlikely to be the safest or most effective option for emergency isolation.

69. The potential for a major accident will depend on a range of factors including:

   - the nature and properties of the substance;
   - the quantity of substance released;
   - the size and nature of populations at risk and their proximity to the plant; and
   - the presence of other plant including confining structures and other hazardous inventories (escalation potential).

70. Ultimately the decision whether or not to provide remote isolation is based on an assessment of:

   - the likelihood that the major accident will occur;
   - the consequences (in terms of the **extent and severity** of harm to people).

71. Together these factors represent the risk. The reduction in risk is the benefit that must be balanced against the cost of providing the facility.

Benefits of ROSOVs

Toxic hazards

72. For toxic hazards ROSOVs can have a significant benefit by reducing the extent of the hazard so that fewer people are exposed. However, since the ROSOV may fail on demand, the risk is reduced but not eliminated.

73. Also, people on site may be within the hazard range irrespective of whether the release is terminated rapidly by a ROSOV or is more prolonged due to reliance on manual isolation. However, even in these cases, terminating the release more rapidly will reduce their exposure.

74. Providing a remote (or automatic) activation facility will avoid employees having to deliberately enter a toxic atmosphere to effect isolation manually.

Flammable hazards

75. For flammable substances, employees should not be required to deliberately enter a flammable atmosphere to isolate plant manually, especially as personal protective equipment (PPE), is not a practicable solution.

76. The potential for escalation is much greater for flammable substances, particularly in complex plant with significant areas of congestion due to closely spaced plant, pipework and other structures. When ignition occurs in a congested area there is an increased risk of a vapour cloud explosion. The overpressure from a vapour cloud explosion may be capable of critically damaging other plant, leading to further loss of containment and potential casualties.

Personal protective equipment

77. In accordance with the hierarchy of measures described in the *Control of Substances Hazardous to Health Regulations* (COSHH),[12] provision of personal protective equipment (PPE) is not considered an adequate alternative to remote isolation for a new installation for which fitting ROSOVs is considered reasonably practicable.

78. For existing installations, the practice of manual isolation by employees wearing PPE should only be adopted if the cost of retrofitting ROSOVs is grossly disproportionate to the reduction in risk.

Bunding

79. Secondary containment in the form of a bund is a measure to mitigate the consequences of a spill once it has occurred, and therefore comes lower in the hierarchy of controls than measures that limit the loss of material from the primary containment system.

80. A bund may be required to contain a range of potential releases for which a ROSOV would not be capable – including, for example, overflowing of a vessel and holes in the vessel itself. ROSOVs and secondary containment are not mutually exclusive and both may be required to reduce the risks from the range of possible hazardous events to ALARP.

81. For a new installation, priority should be given to reasonably practicable measures to prevent the escape of the hazardous substance from the primary containment system (vessel, pump, pipework etc) over the provision of secondary containment.

82. For existing installations where secondary containment is already provided, the consequences of a release within the bunded area will be mitigated. This can be taken into account when making decisions about the reasonable practicability of retrofitting a ROSOV.

83. However, where the pipework extends beyond the bunded area, the principal benefits offered by the bund will be lost in the event of a failure outside. The bund wall may limit encroachment of the spillage on the vessel(s) within the bund, but the resulting pool will be potentially much larger and may spread to other vulnerable locations.

84. Where the hazardous substance is under pressure, eg being pumped, then some failures that take place within the bund could result in a jet or spray of the fluid being projected beyond the confines of the secondary containment. This is particularly true for some poorly designed or inadequately maintained bunds.

85. Even for releases into the bund, bunding does nothing to limit the size of the release but limits the size of the pool and hence the evaporation rate. The evaporation rate will reach a maximum once the quantity of material released is sufficient to cover the area of the bund. This is irrespective of whether the release is isolated manually or remotely. However, a longer release means more material transferred into the bund. Unless steps are taken to control evaporation from the liquid in the bund, eg by covering the surface with an inert barrier, the evaporation will continue for a longer period with potentially adverse results. For example, if a flammable substance is released into the bund and ignited, the larger quantity of fuel is likely to result in a more prolonged fire, increasing the risk of escalation.

Dual hazard substances and mixtures

86. Some substances may be both toxic and flammable and while their CHIP classification usually reflects the greater hazard, in some circumstances the secondary hazard may dominate. For substances with both flammable and toxic properties the selection criteria should be applied for each hazard separately and if different standards are indicated then the higher standard should be adopted.

87. In the case of simple mixtures of substances within the scope of this guidance a similar approach may be taken, with the standard adopted being the highest required for each of the components.

88. If one component is a minor constituent, eg a small percentage of a toxic substance in a flammable solvent, then you should refer to Schedule 3 of the CHIP Regulations and the *Approved Classification and Labelling Guide*[6] to arrive at an appropriate categorisation.

89. In some cases the substance may have a secondary hazard category that falls outside of the scope of this guidance, eg for oxidisers or substances that react with water. The secondary property should be separately assessed, by reference to other relevant good practice or by means of a case-specific assessment, and again the higher standard should be adopted (see Appendix 1).

The selection criteria

How do the selection criteria work?

90. To help you decide whether to use a ROSOV in a particular case, a number of selection criteria have been developed based on judgements about the extent and severity of the consequences in the event of a major accident.

91. The criteria are divided into two groups of primary and secondary selection criteria.

92. Primary selection criteria serve to quickly eliminate low-risk cases where the hazard potential is sufficiently low that the provision of remote isolation is unlikely to be justified.

93. Where it can be shown that **all** of the primary selection criteria are satisfied, then a ROSOV would not normally be required.

94. When you apply the primary selection criteria and they do not eliminate the need for a ROSOV, you should choose either to provide a ROSOV or alternatively to refine the assessment by applying the secondary criteria.

95. The secondary selection criteria identify a series of generic circumstances in which the hazards are considered to be so significant that you should normally fit ROSOVs when any one or more of these criteria apply.

96. This second group of criteria are more detailed and require a deeper analysis of the potential consequences of a loss of containment event. If you can show that none of the secondary selection criteria are applicable then a ROSOV is unlikely to be a reasonably practicable measure.

97. If the application of the selection criteria does not eliminate the need for a ROSOV then provision of a ROSOV is considered to be good practice for a new installation.

98. For an existing installation, a ROSOV should normally be fitted unless a sufficiently detailed analysis is made to show that retrofitting is not reasonably practicable in the circumstances.

99. Appendix 1 gives guidance on the factors that you will need to consider in a case-specific assessment if it is to be accepted as a suitable and sufficient demonstration.

Event frequencies

100. There is considerable difficulty and uncertainty associated with determining the frequency of loss of containment events. This guidance employs simplified decision criteria in which greater emphasis is placed on the scale of the potential release and the severity of the potential consequences than on the frequency. If you choose to employ frequency-based arguments you should be prepared to provide a robust justification for the frequencies used.

The primary selection criteria

101. The following are the primary selection criteria:

- The maximum foreseeable release of a hazardous substance in the event of failure to isolate manually is less than 1% of the controlled quantity (Q) specified in Schedule 1, Column 2 of the Planning (Control of Major Accident Hazards) Regulations 1995 for the purposes of Hazardous Substances Consent for the named substance (Part A), or category of substance (Part B).
- Manual isolation would not require employees to enter a flammable atmosphere and expose them to risk of serious personal injury or death during the attempt.
- Manual isolation would not require employees to enter an area in which the concentration of a toxic substance exceeds a level at which a normal healthy individual could escape unaided and would not put them at risk of serious personal injury or death while attempting the isolation.
- The rate and duration of the release is such that no potential for serious danger (death or serious injury – ie injury requiring an overnight stay in hospital) can be foreseen.

The secondary selection criteria

102. If you find that the primary selection criteria do not rule out the need for a ROSOV then the following secondary criteria should be used and a ROSOV fitted when one or more of these criteria apply:

- A ROSOV is required by other relevant and authoritative guidance on good practice, eg substance or process specific guidance such as *Safety advice for bulk chlorine installations*[13] or the Liquefied Petroleum Gases Association Codes of Practice.
- The hazardous substance is present as a gas liquefied under pressure and the circumstances under which ROSOVs should be fitted are not already dealt with in existing substance or process specific and authoritative guidance on good practice.
- The valve serves to isolate a flexible loading arm, hose or similar vulnerable item of plant where there are frequent connections and disconnections.
- The location of the potential loss of containment is outside of any bunded area or other secondary containment.
- Failure to isolate a release of a flammable substance, the direct consequences of which (eg thermal radiation or overpressure) are confined to the site, could result in escalation involving a release of another hazardous substance with off-site consequences.
- The extended release duration associated with manual isolation (likely to be at least 20 minutes) results in an increased number of predicted off-site fatalities when compared to the case with a ROSOV.

Selection and operation of ROSOVs

Activation

103. ROSOVs can be manually activated through push buttons located a distance from the valve. Automatic shutoff valves (ASOVs) activated by a detection system, eg a toxic or flammable gas detector, can provide a more immediate response.

Manual activation

104. One advantage of manual activation is that an intelligent assessment of the most appropriate measure for dealing with a release can be made. Claims are sometimes made that manual activation is necessary to avoid spurious trips associated with automatic systems; however, the root cause is often a badly designed system rather than any inherent weakness in an automated response.

105. Manual activation must be justifiable and the location of push buttons must not endanger the employee. They should be accessible and in a safe and suitable place in relation to the hazardous event that may occur. There should normally be at least two alternate activation points, which should be readily identifiable both on the plant (eg labelling) and in all relevant operating instructions.

ASOVs

106. Advantages of ASOVs include more rapid isolation and a reduction in the frequency of some modes of human error.

107. Facilities for manual activation, on emergency escape routes for example, should be provided as a backup to automatic activation and can result in a more rapid response in some circumstances.

Types of valves

108. The detailed selection of a particular valve, including materials of construction, is beyond the scope of this guidance and advice should be sought from your supplier or manufacturer. A key feature of any valve used for emergency isolation is the ability to achieve and maintain tight shutoff within an appropriate timescale. Commonly used valve types include gate valves and plug valves. But it is important that each valve is chosen to meet the specific requirements of your installation.

Actuators

109. A remotely operated valve can be operated by a variety of different methods such as pneumatic, hydraulic or electrical energy sources. ROSOVs should continue to be capable of performing their function in the event of failure of the primary power supply, eg mechanical springs or pressurised fluid reservoirs.

110. It may be possible to convert existing manual isolation valves to remote operation by incorporating an actuator and a suitable control system. The suitability of such a conversion is beyond the scope of this guidance and advice should be sought from the manufacturer of the valve and/or the actuator.

111. The correct sizing of the actuator is crucial to meeting the safety requirements specification of the ROSOV. Undersizing may result in the valve not operating on demand while oversizing may result in damage to the valve or actuator assembly. The design must show an understanding of the safety requirements and be based on the complete system characteristics. This would include taking into account:

- the static/dynamic forces of the assembly;
- the effect of the process application on these forces;
- the frequency of exercising the system;
- the minimum/maximum range of gas/hydraulic pressures used for actuation; and
- the fact that actuators are manufactured in discrete sizes.

112. The competence required to carry out a successful system design may not reside in a single organisation (eg if the actuator and valve come from different suppliers). However, overall responsibility for the complete system meeting its safety requirements specification should be clearly assigned.

Failure mode

113. Most ROSOVs provided for emergency isolation are generally configured to close, and so isolate the hazardous inventory, on failure. However, it should not be automatically assumed that this results in a safe condition in all cases. If the ability to reopen the isolation valve following the initial shutdown (eg due to loss of utilities) is critical to safety, then backup supplies should be provided.

External hazards

114. ROSOVs should be protected against external hazards such as fires or explosions to ensure that:

   - they can be closed; and
   - they will continue to provide tight shutoff.

Consequential hazards

115. The benefits of ROSOVs are clear, but it is important to recognise and address a number of new hazards that may arise as a consequence of their installation. Some of the risk reduction provided by the ROSOV may be offset by risks associated with the installation and ongoing maintenance. The need for additional measures to tackle these consequential hazards should not be taken as a bar to fitting ROSOVs, but may influence the reasonable practicability of retrofitting ROSOVs to an existing installation. Examples of some of these consequential hazards are listed below.

116. On complex or interconnecting plant, the location of ROSOVs needs careful consideration due to the potential for:

   - over pressurisation due to 'blocking in' a liquid with a high expansion coefficient; and
   - the effects of spurious valve operation.

117. Other potential hazards associated with isolation valves include:

   - the creation of damaging pressure surges ('hammer') in long pipe runs if valves close too quickly;
   - introduction of a new potential leak source;
   - hazards associated with installation, maintenance and testing; and
   - general increase in complexity of the system.

Dual function valves

118. In some cases, the normal process control system includes valves, activated by process measurement sensors and acting as part of a trip or shutdown system.

119. Emergency isolation valves need to be capable of achieving and maintaining tight shutoff. Some types of control valves are designed to provide a 'throttling' action and this type do not always provide a sufficiently tight seal. Other types of valve used, eg in the control of batch transfers, may be capable of achieving a tight seal. Failure of a dual function valve may compromise both functions and a postulated failure of the control valve may itself lead to a requirement for an emergency isolation valve.

120. Therefore, the functions of process control and emergency isolation should normally be kept separate. Ultimately, the test will be whether the control system can deliver the required safety integrity level with a dual function valve.

121. Further advice on control system integrity can be found in British Standards EN61508 *Functional safety of electrical/electronic/programmable electronic safety-related systems* and IEC61511 *Functional safety: safety instrumented systems for the process industry sector*.

Excess flow valves

122. An excess flow valve is designed to remain open in normal operation, but if the flow through the valve exceeds a preset maximum, the valve closes. These valves allow flow in either direction, but normally only trigger for excess flow in the specified flow direction. The valve setting must exceed the maximum flow rate foreseeable in normal operation. Depending on the particular design of valve a setting significantly higher (perhaps as much as 50%) may be required to avoid 'chatter' and damage to the valve.

123. A catastrophic failure downstream of the valve will result in increased flow and a pressure drop across the valve, causing it to close. Where the downstream failure is more limited, eg a hole or a crack, or there is crushing of the pipework then the restricted flow may not be sufficient to cause the valve to shut and the release will continue.

124. Other factors are relevant when considering use of an excess flow valve. Foreign matter can lodge in the valve and prevent it from closing. In some applications it can be difficult to simulate the excess flow condition for proof testing.

125. Advantages claimed for excess flow valves include the relative simplicity of a mechanical system and their automatic action – eliminating some potential human errors. In the context of this guidance excess flow valves would not normally be considered equivalent to ROSOVs for emergency isolation. Many of the same issues surrounding retrofitting apply, but in some cases lower costs overall may mean that an excess flow valve is reasonably practicable to retrofit when a ROSOV is not.

Vulnerable vessel fittings

126. Process equipment may include small-bore connections for items such as control system components. Some of these, eg for level instrumentation, may enter below the liquid level in the vessel. Failure could, therefore, result in loss of the vessel contents. Fittings of this type may be most vulnerable to guillotine failure (being sheared off). An excess flow valve, preferably located in the outlet, but in any case as close to the vessel as practicable, may be an acceptable alternative to a ROSOV for this type of application.

127. Detailed advice on the selection, installation and maintenance of excess flow valves is beyond the scope of this guidance. Advice should be sought from your supplier or manufacturer.

Reliability and integrity

128. Any control system can fail. Proper maintenance and regular proof testing of valves make a major contribution to maintaining valve integrity.

129. Examples of potential failure modes are considered below. If you establish how systems can fail it provides useful information for inclusion in testing and maintenance arrangements. Common factors identified in previous industrial incidents where isolation systems failed include:

- failure to close on demand due to inadequate maintenance/proof testing;
- failure to shut tight leading to leakage internally due to incorrect specification of the valve or inadequate maintenance/proof testing;
- failure of employees to activate a serviceable valve due to inadequate training and/or unclear instructions;
- large volumes released after 'successful' isolation due to inappropriate spacing between isolation valves;
- valves rendered unserviceable by the incident, eg damaged by fire or explosion; and
- failure-to-danger of valve on loss of motive power.

Inspection and proof testing

130. You should put in place appropriate arrangements for inspection and proof testing to reduce the likelihood of the ROSOV to fail to operate effectively on demand, to ALARP.

131. The frequency of inspection and testing required will depend to a great extent on the confidence held in the compatibility of the valve with the process fluids and conditions. This confidence may be obtained through previous operational experience, testing, knowledge of basic materials compatibility or a combination of these.

132. The lower the level of confidence the more frequent should be the inspection and testing of the valve. Records of these early inspections and tests will provide the basis of a justification for increased test and inspection intervals as operational experience is accrued.

Appendix 1 A case-specific assessment of the reasonable practicability of a ROSOV

Introduction

This appendix gives guidance on how to determine whether a ROSOV is a reasonably practicable measure to mitigate the consequences of a loss of containment of a hazardous substance. It is limited to a consideration of the potential for harm to human health.

Should a loss of containment occur the nature of the hazardous substance and the processing conditions would have a major bearing on the consequences, and so strongly influence the decision to incorporate remote isolation facilities.

A case-specific assessment of reasonable practicability requires that each installation be assessed individually, taking account of its specific design features, safety systems and operating procedures.

Process

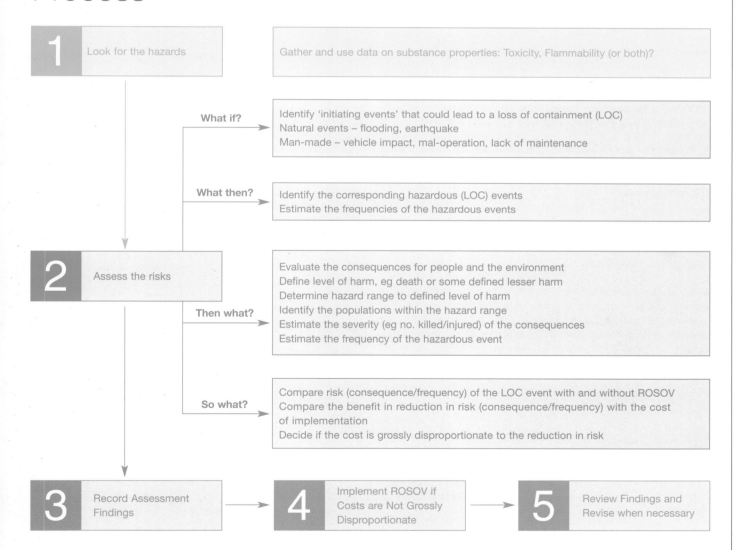

1 Look for the hazards

Gather and use data on substance properties: Toxicity, Flammability (or both)?

What if?
Identify 'initiating events' that could lead to a loss of containment (LOC)
Natural events – flooding, earthquake
Man-made – vehicle impact, mal-operation, lack of maintenance

What then?
Identify the corresponding hazardous (LOC) events
Estimate the frequencies of the hazardous events

2 Assess the risks

Then what?
Evaluate the consequences for people and the environment
Define level of harm, eg death or some defined lesser harm
Determine hazard range to defined level of harm
Identify the populations within the hazard range
Estimate the severity (eg no. killed/injured) of the consequences
Estimate the frequency of the hazardous event

So what?
Compare risk (consequence/frequency) of the LOC event with and without ROSOV
Compare the benefit in reduction in risk (consequence/frequency) with the cost of implementation
Decide if the cost is grossly disproportionate to the reduction in risk

3 Record Assessment Findings

4 Implement ROSOV if Costs are Not Grossly Disproportionate

5 Review Findings and Revise when necessary

The flowchart above illustrates the process of assessment in the context of ROSOVs.

Stage 1:
Look for the hazards

Introduction

The first stage of the assessment is to identify and understand the hazardous properties of the substances under review. Information on the hazards of a particular substance may be obtained from a variety of sources. The foremost of these is the Material Safety Data Sheet, which should be issued by the supplier of the substance in accordance with the *Chemicals (Hazard Information and Packaging for Supply) Regulations 2002* (SI1689).[6] An indication of the primary hazard of a substance can be obtained from the CHIP classification.

Dual hazard substances

Some substances may be both toxic and flammable. While the CHIP classification usually reflects the greater hazard, in some circumstances the secondary hazard may dominate. For substances with both flammable and toxic properties you should apply the criteria for each hazard separately. If different standards are indicated then the higher standard should be adopted.

In the case of simple mixtures of substances within the scope of this guidance, a similar approach may be taken. The standard adopted should be the highest required for each of the components.

If one component is a minor constituent, eg a small percentage of a toxic substance in a flammable solvent, then you can use the CHIP methodology to arrive at an appropriate categorisation.

In some cases the substance may have a secondary hazard outside of the scope of this guidance, eg for oxidisers or substances that react with water. You should assess the secondary property separately, by reference to other relevant good practice or by means of a case-specific assessment, and again adopt the higher standard.

Toxic substances

Toxic substances tend to have longer hazard ranges and greater potential to affect larger, more remote populations beyond the site boundary. Thermal radiation and overpressure effects following ignited releases of flammable substances are more likely to result in damage to other plant, and hence to escalation, than are toxic releases.

However, there is the potential for personnel exposed to a toxic substance to be rendered incapable of controlling or shutting down plant safely. This can lead to further incidents and escalation. Vulnerable occupied buildings including Control Rooms should be identified as part of an Occupied Buildings Assessment for the establishment. The Chemical Industries Association publication *Guidance for the Location and Design of Occupied Buildings on Chemical Manufacturing Sites*,[15] contains useful advice on this topic.

A ROSOV may reduce both the risk of harm due to direct exposure to the toxic substance and the likelihood of escalation of the event as a result of employees being unable to perform essential duties.

Routes into the human body include inhalation, ingestion and via contact with the skin. The primary route of harm following a loss of containment event is inhalation. But there will also be the possibility of exposure via other routes during clean-up operations.

Flammable substances

The hazard ranges associated with fires and explosions following the release and ignition of a flammable substance tend to be shorter than for toxic substances, and may be confined to the site. However, with flammable substances there is greater potential for escalation due to the effects of thermal radiation and/or overpressure on other items of plant causing further loss of containment.

Other properties

Other properties of substances in addition to toxicity and flammability can have a significant impact on the risk. A toxic substance with a higher vapour pressure, for example, will disperse more readily and to a greater hazard range from the point of release.

Processing or storage conditions

The conditions under which the substance is stored and/or processed can also be a significant factor.

Liquids classified as Flammable, but with flashpoints above ambient temperature, generally present a lower hazard than those classified as Highly Flammable liquids. However, storage or processing at elevated temperatures can result in these substances being released above their flashpoints or even their auto-ignition temperatures.

Substances that are gases at ambient temperature are frequently stored as liquids under pressure. Releases from pressurised storage are more energetic. For a given hole size, a greater mass of substance will be released per unit time, particularly if the substance is released in the liquid phase.

Inventory and scale of release

Process plant typically consists of a series of larger containments such as vessels, columns etc joined by pipework, flanges, pumps, heat exchangers etc. Failures are most likely to occur in and around these interconnecting items, which often (though not always) contain relatively small quantities of substances themselves. But, if there is no effective (safe) means to isolate a leak from say a pump, then the contents of the larger containment item may be lost.

It is important, therefore, to consider containment systems as a whole and not just as individual vessels. Boundaries need to be set between units of inventory. Appropriate means of isolation, which may include ROSOVs, should be provided between individual inventory units to limit the quantity of substance that can be released from any single failure. Incidents have occurred in which ROSOVs were provided and functioned correctly; however the quantity of substance between isolations was too large and a significant release still took place.

The nature and scale of an emergency is often determined by the rate at which a hazardous substance is released rather than simply the bulk inventory. It is this rate of release that determines the size of the liquid pool or the flammable gas cloud formed, or the length and diameter of a jet flame. Factors influencing the rate of release include the pressure and the area of the breach – all other things being equal, the greater the pressure and/or the larger the bore of the pipework, the greater the release rate. That said, larger bore pipework tends to be less vulnerable to some of the possible failure modes, eg impact. To an extent, the consequences and frequency may balance each other out.

Stage 2:
Assess the risks

Introduction

A risk assessment considers a range of possible adverse events and evaluates both the likelihood of the event and the magnitude of the potential consequences. In this context, the frequency and the consequences of the event, taken together, describe the risk associated with that event.

A judgement is then made regarding the tolerability of the risk, and the reasonable practicability of risk reduction options, by comparison with suitable criteria.

Degree of quantification

Risk assessments may be made with varying degrees of rigour or quantification, and each of the elements of a risk assessment is subject to varying degrees of uncertainty.

In some cases, professional judgement alone may be used to assign event frequencies on a qualitative basis. In others, a more detailed analysis of the possible causes of a failure using techniques including fault trees may be made to quantify the failure rate more precisely.

The consequences of an event are frequently better characterised than the frequency. It is common to quantify the consequences of a given event and pair the result with a qualitative judgement as to the likelihood.

If a clear and unambiguous decision can be made then this level of quantification is likely to be adequate. If, due to uncertainties in the data or the assumptions made in the analysis, it is not clear whether or not fitting a ROSOV is a reasonably practicable option, then further quantification may be required.

In all cases, the degree of quantification required will be that necessary to justify the decision taken. You should test the sensitivity of your analysis to any assumptions made, eg about event frequency or about similar factors in the consequence assessment.

Definition: quantified risk assessment

Ultimately, the consequences and frequencies of the range of possible events may be fully quantified and combined into a single risk value or relationship.

Iso-contours of individual risk can be used to determine at what distance and in which direction a threshold risk is reached for the purposes of comparison with tolerability criteria.

In making judgements about the reasonable practicability of a particular safety measure, it is also necessary to consider 'societal' or 'group' risk – which is essentially the risk of harm to multiple individuals as the result of the same hazardous event.

The use of numerical risk estimates in this manner is commonly referred to as a Quantified Risk Assessment (QRA). It will not always be necessary, or even helpful, to perform a full QRA. In many cases the results of a qualitative assessment will be sufficiently clear to allow a decision to be made.

Steps in risk assessment

The separate steps in a risk assessment have been described more memorably as

What if..., What then..., Then what... and So what...

Step one

What if...

Introduction

The first step is to identify the potential causes or 'initiating events' of a loss of containment event. These can be split into two broad categories of event: those arising from external events such as seismic activity or flooding, and on-site events including failures due to corrosion, vehicular impact or mal-operation.

Equipment failures

All plant items have a set of unique failure modes, some of which can lead to a loss of containment. A review of each failure will serve to identify if a serious risk is present.

It is important to establish those site-specific failure modes whose consequences would require isolation.

Some equipment failures may have no significant effect, warranting only minor maintenance attention such as adjustment or resetting. Others, such as seal failures or equipment failing to operate, may have much more serious consequences. Identification of the critical failure modes of the plant equipment is best achieved through direct operating knowledge and experience.

Plant maintenance records can be used to identify equipment that may give rise to a loss of containment incident. Generic information, from published sources or held centrally within a company, can be useful but will not take account of local conditions which will affect the performance of equipment. Other sources of information include reports from Hazard and Operability (HAZOP) studies and reviews of Pipework and Instrumentation Diagrams (PID).

Table 1 gives some examples of typical equipment failures.

Table 1 Typical Equipment Failures

Equipment	Principal Failure Modes	Principal Failure Causes
Pipework	Holes and ruptures	Corrosion, erosion, cavitation, impact, vibration, 'hammer'
Pipework, grants, flanged connections	Leaks	Deterioration of material, wrong gasket used, incorrect assembly of joint
Instrumentation connection (small base tube)	Ruptures and disconnections	Impact, vibration, incorrect fitting, incorrect make up
Flexible hoses	Holes, ruptures, disconnections	Fatigue, impact damage, misuse, poor connection, mechanical failures
Valves	External leak	Gland seal, jointed faces
Pumps	External leak	Drive shaft, apping, flanged faces, chainlocks
Compressors	Leaks, seals, flanged faces, soiled connections, drains	Vibration, perished joint material, operator error, leak past seat
Drain and simple points	Leaks at seals and flanged faces, valve left open, full bore ruptures	Perished joint material, operator error, impact

What if...

▶
Initiating event frequencies

It may be necessary to estimate the frequency of the initiating events if these are to be used to estimate the overall frequency of the hazardous event (loss of containment). Alternatively, frequencies of hazardous events may be assigned based on historical data provided this is available and relevant.

Definition: external events

An external event is one that has no direct relationship with the equipment, but which is capable of acting on the equipment causing it to fail.

This includes all natural phenomena such as earthquakes, high winds, flooding etc. Interference by third parties engaged in vandalism or theft may be relevant. It includes those activities that may be going on around the plant such as the movement of road vehicles or lifting

operations, ie the potential for impact damage. Also included are incidents on adjacent plant that could escalate, affecting the plant under consideration, ie the 'domino effect'.

Definition: human factors

In many cases, accidents and incidents are attributed to human failure. These can include unintentional errors such as mistakenly starting a pump, opening the wrong valve, or failing to replace a seal. Sometimes custom and practice procedural shortcuts can contribute to human failures.

Further guidance is available in the publication *Reducing error and influencing behaviour*.[16]

Influences on human failure

The table below gives some influences that increase the likelihood of human failure.

▶

Table 2 Influences on Human Failure

Job Factors	Illogical design of equipment and instruments
	Constant interruptions
	Information hard to find or assimilate
	Missing or unclear instructions
	Poorly maintained or unreliable equipment
	High workload, time pressure
	Noisy and unpleasant working conditions
Individual Factors	Low skill and competence
	Tired staff
	Bored or disheartened staff
	Individual medical problems
Organisational Factors	Poor work planning leading to high work pressure
	Poor communications
	Uncertainties in roles and responsibilities
	Poor management of health and safety
	Inadequate staffing level
	Inadequate training – routine emergency operations
	Inadequate supervision

Step one

What if...

What if analysis for human factors

The What if... analysis should identify those tasks where human failures could arise. Analysis is usually done by structured task and error analysis methods. Involvement of operators in the analysis is essential to provide a 'reality check' of what is actually done on the plant and what steps are feasible. Such analysis is preferable to just relying on what is written in the operating procedure.

Key tasks

Key tasks to consider include:

- normal operating duties;
- sampling tasks;
- venting/draining;
- connecting/disconnecting;
- start up/shut down;
- cleaning and maintenance;
- emergency response.

Probability estimates

Methods are available to allow the estimation of human error probabilities. However, this should be done with extreme caution to ensure that estimates are appropriate for the nature of the task and the site-specific conditions.

Response times

Particular care is needed when estimating the likely time for operators to respond to an incident. Consideration should be given to the detection, diagnosis and action stages of response.

Detection

How an operator will become aware that a problem exists. Assessment of alarm priorities and frequencies, the characteristics of the operator console displays, as well as operators' past experience of similar problems on sites are all useful aspects to review. Plant problems that appear over a period of time, and where the information available to the operators can be uncertain, are particularly difficult to detect. When Control Rooms are not continually staffed you need to be able to show that plant problems can still be detected quickly and reliably.

Diagnosis

How an operator will determine what action, if any, is required to respond to the problem. Training and competence assurance, the availability of clear operating procedures and other job aids, and the level of supervision are all relevant factors to think about. The existence of more than one problem can make diagnosis more difficult.

Action

This stage covers how a timely response is carried out. Key aspects here include:

- a reliable means of communicating with other plant operators;
- time to locate and operate the correct isolation valve;
- for manual isolation valves, consider the need to don PPE and the potential difficulty in operating the valve whilst wearing PPE;
- for remotely operated valves, feedback needs to be given to operators that the valve has operated correctly;
- consider that operators may hesitate if operating the valve leads to criticism later.

A 'walk-through' of the physical aspects of the task with operators can provide very useful information on the minimum time needed to operate an isolation valve. However, an allowance for additional delays due to uncertainty, hesitation, communications problems and so on should be added for a realistic estimate of the response time.

Additional guidance is available in these publications (available on the HSE website at www.hse.gov.uk):

Better alarm handling HSE Information Sheet

Human factors aspects of remote operation in process plants

Assessing the safety of staffing arrangements for process operations in the chemical and allied industries

Human factors integration: implementation in the onshore and offshore industries ▶

Step two

What then...

Introduction

The second step is to identify those initiating events that contribute to the hazardous event under consideration – the event that would be mitigated by isolation.

Hazardous events

A given hazardous event might have several potential initiators. For example, both corrosion and impact might be causes of a pipework failure. Similarly, each initiating event could lead to several hazardous events. Some of these may be effectively mitigated by a ROSOV, eg failure of pipework due to corrosion, whilst others will not, eg a corrosion-induced hole in a storage tank.

Frequency of hazardous event

The procedure for tracing initiating events through to hazardous events can be made easier by the use of logic trees. This form of analysis can be used to generate frequencies for the hazardous events.

However, there can be considerable difficulties in practice and it is easy to overlook initiating events and hence underestimate the frequency of the hazardous event. This is why it is common to turn to an analysis of historical data.

Step three

Then what...

Introduction

The third step is to evaluate the consequences of the identified hazardous event or loss of containment. This process involves predicting the behaviour of the hazardous material once released from containment, in order to determine how the concentration of the substance will vary with distance from the release point.

To be capable of causing a major accident, toxic substances must be present in a physical form such that dispersion is possible in the conditions that exist at the time of the accident.

For flammable substances, ignition (with consequent thermal and/or overpressure effects) can occur close to the source of the release after minimal dispersion. But in some cases a cloud of flammable vapour may drift some distance away from the release point (where ignition sources may be strictly controlled) before finding a source of ignition.

In the context of this guidance, we are generally concerned with releases of gaseous or volatile liquid substances, which can become airborne, and be transported some distance from the point of release. However, even substances with relatively low vapour pressures can form a flammable or toxic cloud, if for example they are released under pressure, forming a spray or mist.

For toxic substances, the extent of the hazard is related to the concentration of the substance to which those affected are exposed. Critical factors in determining the degree of harm include the concentration and the exposure time – collectively known as 'the dose'.

For flammable substances, the hazard is again related to the concentration. But the hazard will only be realised if the concentration is within certain critical limits and there is a source of ignition. Some initiating events may simultaneously provide a source of ignition, eg in the event of a release due to vehicular impact there are also likely to be sparks and/or hot vehicle components present.

Definition: source term

A source term describes the conditions (eg temperature and pressure) and other critical parameters, including release rate and the physical properties of the substance that together define the release.

Take, for example, a gas liquefied under pressure. For a given sized hole in the containment barrier, the source term depends on whether the substance is released as a liquid, eg from pipework carrying liquid, or as vapour if the failure occurs in pipework connected to the vapour space.

▶

Then what...

Extent of the hazard

From the source term, knowledge of the way substances behave when dispersed into the atmosphere, and the harm criteria, the extent of the harmful effect or the 'hazard range' can be estimated. The hazard range, in conjunction with data on the population at risk, is used to determine the severity of the consequences.

A detailed consideration of the techniques for modelling the dispersion of hazardous substances is beyond the scope of this guidance. At the time this guidance was being prepared, plans were at an advanced stage to make the following HTML-based tool available on HSE's website: 'Guidance on dispersion models for the assessment of COMAH safety cases'.

This work includes general guidance on dispersion modelling, plus reviews of some of the models more frequently employed by duty holders in preparing safety reports submitted under the COMAH Regulations.

Another useful source is the Dutch TNO publication, (the 'Yellow Book'), *Methods for the calculation of the physical effects of the escape of dangerous materials* (see particularly Part 2, Chapter 7 'Dispersion'). C J P van Buijtenen. 1979. 3/L.

Harm criteria

Harm criteria describe the degree of harm, which could be death or some specified lesser harm resulting from exposure to the hazard.

For toxic substances, the harm criteria are commonly expressed in the form of a 'dose', or concentration/time relationship, though other relationships are possible.

For flammable substances, the harm criteria are commonly related to either the effects of exposure to thermal radiation from, for example, pool fires, jet fires or fireballs or, in the event of an explosion, to the overpressure generated.

Harm criteria for overpressure may be related to the direct effects on the human body or, more usually, be indirectly related to the effects of overpressure on structures which may collapse, or to the impact of missiles generated by the explosion. It is more usual to use the indirect relationship to the effects on structures because these can result in harm at significantly lower overpressures.

Secondary containment

It is good practice when designing a new installation to apply a hierarchical approach to the selection of risk reduction measures. ROSOVs (which serve to limit the quantity of substance released from the primary containment) should be installed, if reasonably practicable, in preference to bunding, which serves to minimise the consequences once the material has escaped.

When considering the reasonable practicability of retrofitting ROSOVs to an existing installation, existing measures, including bunding, may be taken into account when establishing the current risk for comparison purposes.

A bund may be required to contain and mitigate a range of potential releases against which a ROSOV would not be effective – including, for example, overflowing of a vessel and holes in the vessel itself. ROSOVs and secondary containment are not mutually exclusive and both may be required to reduce the risks from the range of possible hazardous events to ALARP.

Toxic releases

For un-bunded releases of a toxic liquid at ambient temperature, ignoring cooling effects of evaporation, the source term is proportional to the evaporation rate from the pool. This is dependent on the pool size, which increases as more material is added to the pool. The more rapidly the release is isolated, the less material will be released and the smaller the pool formed. A smaller pool will mean a reduced hazard range.

For a bunded release, the evaporation rate will reach a maximum once the quantity of material released is sufficient to cover the area of the bund. This is irrespective of whether the release is isolated manually or remotely. However, a longer release means more material transferred into the bund. Unless steps are taken to control evaporation from the liquid in the bund, eg by covering the surface with an inert barrier, the evaporation will continue for a longer period. People who are in the plume and unable to escape from it, will be exposed to a given concentration of toxic substance for longer and so accumulate a higher dose.

Flammable releases

For bunded releases of flammable liquids, the greater quantity of fuel accumulated in the bund is likely to result in a more prolonged fire if ignited. Adjacent plant will be exposed to thermal radiation for a longer period, increasing the potential for escalation. Where vessels holding flammable substances share a common bund, 'dwarf walls' or similar should be incorporated to limit the spread of smaller releases.

Step three

Then what...

A long continuous release of vapour from an evaporating pool can lead to the formation of a larger cloud of vapour above the lower flammable limit. This increases the extent of the flash fire hazard.

Escalation

For flammable substances, an important consideration is the potential for escalation or 'domino effects'. For example, a relatively small fire/explosion could have direct effects that are confined to the site. But the fire/explosion could result in loss of containment of a more hazardous substance with the potential for substantial off-site consequences.

In these cases, the true extent of the hazard will be related to the escalation event, which may have a lower event frequency but substantially more serious consequences.

Response time

The response time between the initiating event and the release being isolated can have a significant impact on the extent of the hazard. Even when it is possible to effect a safe manual isolation, the additional time taken to do so can significantly increase the release duration and the hazard range.

ASOVs

A further reduction in response time, with a potential reduction in hazard range, may be achieved if the isolation valve is automatically activated in response to, for

example, a detector. Such an arrangement is referred to as an Automatic Shutoff Valve (ASOV).

Similar considerations apply when judging the reasonable practicability of an ASOV. Although it is important to consider the likelihood and consequence of spurious trips, these are not by themselves a justification for not fitting an ASOV. Spurious trips can be controlled by, for example, the appropriate use of diverse redundant sensors operating on a 'voting' system.

Severity of consequences

In the context of harm to human health, the severity of the consequences is directly related to the number of people who may be killed or injured. Casualties can result from direct exposure to the hazardous substance, or to the effects of thermal radiation/overpressure in the case of flammable hazards.

Data on the populations at risk within the specified hazard range is used to estimate the severity of the consequences, eg the number of persons suffering the specified level of harm.

Directional effects

For some events, particularly toxic releases, the extent of the harm and hence the risk will vary according to direction. Some flammable events, including flash fires, can also be influenced by weather, whilst others, eg explosions, tend to be omni-directional in their effects.

Step four

So what...

Introduction

The final step is to compare the risk (frequency x consequence) of the hazardous event with suitable criteria to determine the tolerability of that risk.

Reducing risks, protecting people: HSE's decision-making process,[3] also available online at www.hse.gov.uk includes a discussion of the risk tolerability criteria developed by HSE (as the regulator).

In the context of this guidance, for risks that fall into the 'Tolerable, If ALARP' region of the risk spectrum (see SFAIRP/ALARP/AMN in the Summary of relevant legal requirements), a ROSOV should be considered as a measure to reduce the risk to ALARP.

Risk reduction

In this context, a ROSOV is a measure that mitigates the consequences of a hazardous event rather than

▶

influencing the frequency of that event. However, it is also true that by limiting the consequences of the primary hazardous event, the presence of a ROSOV may reduce the probability of any associated escalation event(s).

Cost-benefit analysis

In forming judgements about the reasonable practicability of a particular safety measure, it is normal to use death as the criterion for harm. The number of 'statistical fatalities' averted, for which there are accepted monetary equivalents, are considered when evaluating the benefits side of the cost-benefit computation.

Serious injuries averted should also be considered when assessing the benefits of the measure being considered. However, although attempts have been made to establish equivalence factors, eg ten major injuries equal one fatality, there are as yet no generally accepted monetary equivalents for non-lethal injuries.

When deciding whether or not to fit a ROSOV, a comparison is made between the risk with and without the ROSOV, and the reduction in risk is compared to the cost of providing the ROSOV.

Gross disproportion

The implementation of a risk reduction measure such as a ROSOV will involve a cost to the duty holder. Equally, a ROSOV is intended to reduce risk from an operation and

this reduction will bring about a benefit (in terms of lives saved etc), which can be expressed in monetary terms. The ratio of the costs to the benefits can be described as a proportion factor (PF). The generally accepted value of avoiding a statistical fatality is approximately £1 million at the time of writing.

It should also be noted, however, that the benefits might also include the avoidance of such things as environmental clean-up costs, increased insurance premiums, loss of asset value, the costs of increased regulatory interference etc.

The measure to reduce the risk, in this case the ROSOV, should be implemented unless the cost is grossly disproportionate to the reduction in risk (or an equally effective alternative is adopted).

Providing the risk analysis is based on cautious best estimates and the costs are realistic (not needlessly inflated beyond the provision of a fit for purpose solution) then, in the context of major hazards, HSE will use the following as the basis for exercising judgement:

- The proportion factor is at least 1 (and possibly at least 2) for risks which are close to being broadly acceptable risks.
- The proportion factor is at least 10 at the tolerable/unacceptable risk boundary.
- For risks between these levels the proportion factor is a matter of professional judgement, but the disproportion between the costs of preventing a fatality (CPF) and the value of a prevented fatality (VPF) must always be gross for a measure not to be reasonably practical.

Stage 3:
Record the assessment findings

Rationale

The final stage of the assessment process is to document the findings of the assessment and the reasoning behind the decisions taken. There is a legal requirement under the Management of Health and Safety at Work Regulations to document the findings of a risk assessment. In the context of this guidance, it is particularly important that the findings are documented thoroughly when they are used to justify not implementing a ROSOV, where one is identified as good practice by the decision criteria presented in this document.

Stage 4:
Implement ROSOV where reasonably practicable

Comment

Where the conclusion of the assessment is that a ROSOV (or, where applicable, another equally effective measure) is reasonably practicable, then implementation should follow as a logical consequence.

Stage 5:
Review the assessment periodically

Introduction

Assessment is not a once-and-for-all activity. With the passage of time, changes in local circumstances and advances in technology etc may alter the conclusions of the risk assessment. For example, an increase in the size of the local population or a decrease in the cost of providing remote isolation may make fitment of a ROSOV a reasonably practicable option where previously it was not.

Significant change

In accordance with the Management of Health and Safety at Work Regulations, duty holders should review and, if necessary, modify their assessment if there is reason to believe that it is no longer valid or if there is a significant change (eg an increase in the population at risk) in the matters to which it relates.

It is prudent in most cases to plan to review risk assessments at regular intervals. There is an explicit requirement (regulation 8) for the Operators of installations subject to the Top Tier requirements of COMAH to review their safety report at least once every five years, or whenever necessary, to take into account new facts or knowledge that becomes available. This should be considered indicative of Good Practice for Operators of other establishments handling hazardous substances.

Appendix 2
Summary of relevant legal requirements

Health and Safety at Work etc Act

1. *The Health and Safety at Work etc Act 1974* places a duty on employers to ensure 'so far as is reasonably practicable' (SFAIRP) the health, safety and welfare at work of their employees, and a duty on employers and the self-employed to ensure that persons other than their employees (including, in the case of the self-employed, themselves) are protected from risks to their health or safety arising from the work activities.

Management of Health and Safety at Work Regulations

2. *The Management of Health and Safety at Work Regulations 1999* (SI 3242) require employers (and where relevant the self-employed) to make a suitable and sufficient assessment of the risks to their employees and to persons who are not their employees but who may be subject to risks arising from the work activities.

Control of Major Accident Hazards Regulations

3. Regulation 4 of the *Control of Major Accident Hazards Regulations 1999* (COMAH) (SI 743) places a duty on the operators of establishments to which the regulations apply to take 'all measures necessary' (AMN) to prevent major accidents and limit their consequences to persons and the environment.

4. Guidance on these regulations can be found in the HSE publication *A guide to the Control of Major Accident Hazard Regulations 1999.* [5]

5. Operators of COMAH establishments (whether 'lower tier' (LT) or 'top tier' (TT)) have a duty to prepare a Major Accident Prevention Policy (MAPP). Operators of COMAH TT sites have an additional duty to submit a safety report to the Competent Authority (CA). The COMAH safety report should demonstrate that the Operator has taken all measures necessary and that the major accident risks have been reduced to ALARP. One of the key demonstrations will be to show that appropriate measures have been taken to prevent and effectively contain releases of dangerous substances.

Dangerous Substances and Explosive Atmospheres Regulations

6. *The Dangerous Substances and Explosive Atmospheres Regulations 2002* (DSEAR) (SI 2776) implement two European Directives: the Chemical Agents Directive (CAD) and the Explosive Atmospheres Directive (ATEX).

7. These regulations deal with fires, explosions and similar energy-releasing events (eg exothermic chemical reactions) arising from dangerous substances (chemical agents) and the explosive atmospheres created by those dangerous substances.

8. DSEAR modernises and repeals over 20 pieces of old safety legislation on flammable substances, dusts and liquids.

References
and useful addresses

1. *The chemical release and fire at the Associated Octel Company Limited: A report of the investigation by the Health and Safety Executive into the chemical release and fire at the Associated Octel Company, Ellesmere Port on 1 and 2 February 1994* Report HSE Books 1996 ISBN 0 7176 0830 1

2. *Emergency isolation of process plant in the chemical industry* Chemical Information Sheet CHIS2 HSE Books 1999

3. *Reducing risks, protecting people: HSE's decision-making process* Report HSE Books 2001 ISBN 0 7176 2151 0

4. *Assessing compliance with the law in individual cases and the use of good practice.* Available on the HSE website: http://www.hse.gov.uk/dst/sctdir.htm#riskassessment

5. *A guide to the Control of Major Accident Hazard Regulations 1999* HSE Books 1999 ISBN 0 7176 1604 5

6. *Approved classification and labelling guide. Chemicals (Hazard Information and Packaging for Supply) Regulations 2002. Guidance on Regulations* L131 (Fifth edition) HSE Books 2002 ISBN 0 7176 2369 6

7. *Approved supply list. Information approved for the classification and labelling of substances and preparations dangerous for supply. Chemicals (Hazard Information and Packaging for Supply) Regulations 2002. Approved list* L129 (Seventh edition) HSE Books 2002 ISBN 0 7176 2368 8

8. *A guide to the Pipelines Safety Regulations 1996* L82 HSE Books ISBN 0 7176 1182 5

9. *The Offshore Installations (Prevention of Fire and Explosion, and Emergency Response) Regulations 1995* The Stationery Office SI 1995 No 743

10. *The safe isolation of plant and equipment* HSE Books 1997 ISBN 0 7176 0871 9

11. *Designing and operating safe chemical reaction processes* HSG143 HSE Books 2000 ISBN 0 7176 1051 9

12. *Control of substances hazardous to health. The Control of Substances Hazardous to Health Regulations 2002. Approved Code of Practice and guidance* L5 (Fourth edition) HSE Books 2002 ISBN 0 7176 2534 6

13. *Safety advice for bulk chlorine installations* HSG28 (Second edition) HSE Books 1999 ISBN 0 7176 1645 2

14. *The Management of Health and Safety at Work Regulations 1999* The Stationery Office SI 3242

15. *Guidance for the location and design of occupied buildings on chemical manufacturing sites* (Second edition) RC21/03 Chemical Industries Association 2003 ISBN 1 85897 114 4 Details on the CIA website at: http://www.cia.org.uk/bookshop/system/index.html

16. *Reducing error and influencing behaviour* HSG48 (Second edition) HSE Books 1999 ISBN 0 7176 2452 8

The Environment Agency

The Environment Agency (England and Wales) has a general enquiry line on 08459 333111 or visit www.environment-agency.gov.uk

The Scottish Environment Protection Agency

For Scotland, the Public Affairs Department of the Scottish Environment Protection Agency, on 01786 457700, handles general enquiries or visit www.sepa.org.uk

While every effort has been made to ensure the accuracy of the references listed in this publication, their future availability cannot be guaranteed.

Printed and published by the Health and Safety Executive   C15   08/04